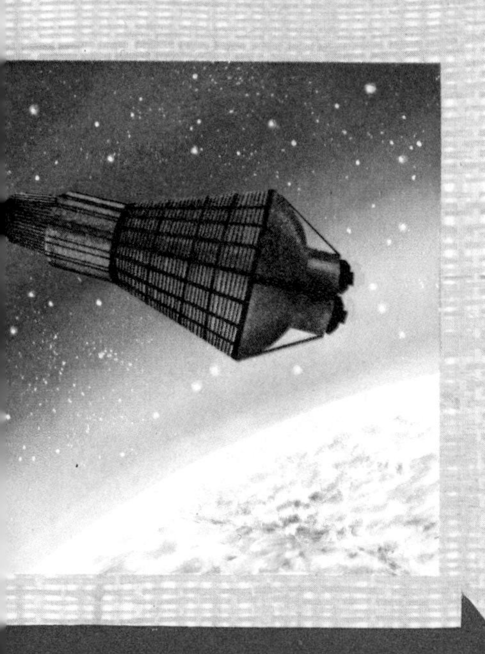

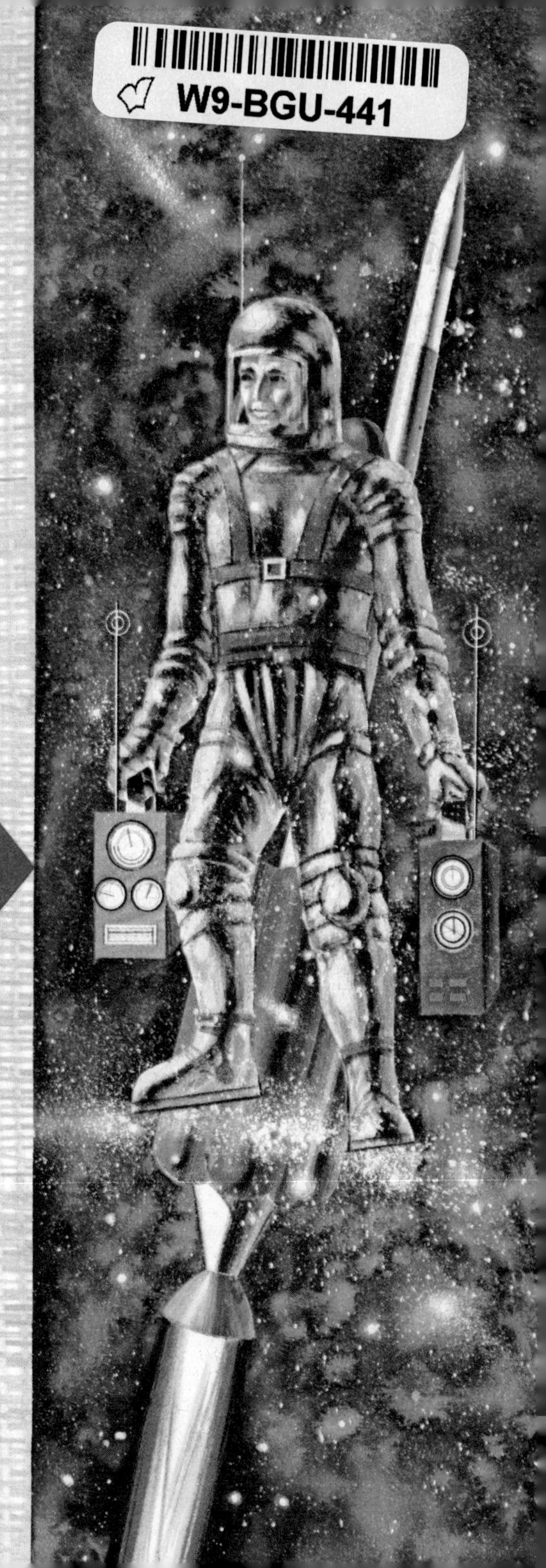

ROCKE

To Explore the

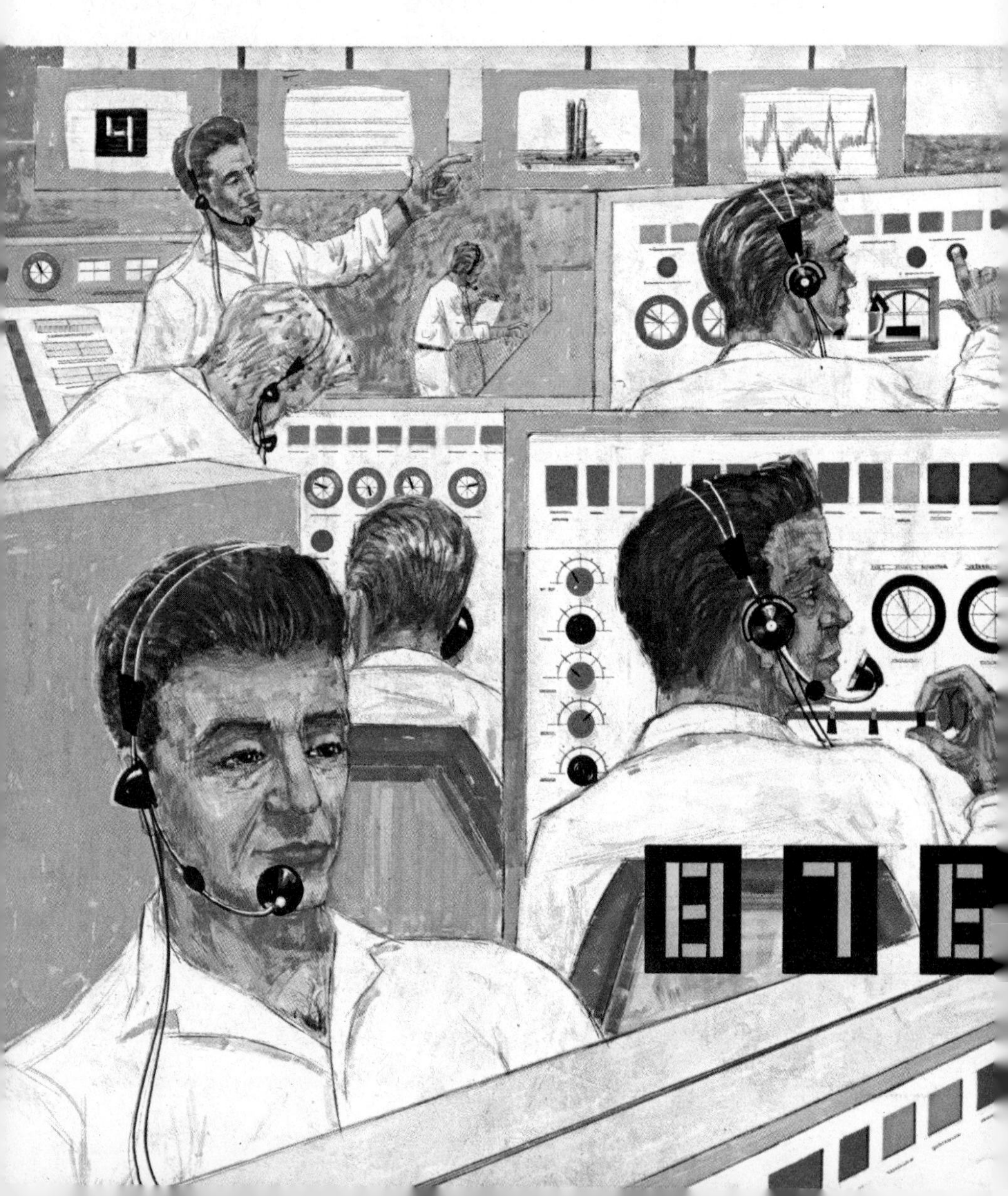

TS

Unknown

by DON E. ROGERS

Illustrated by GEORGE BAKACS

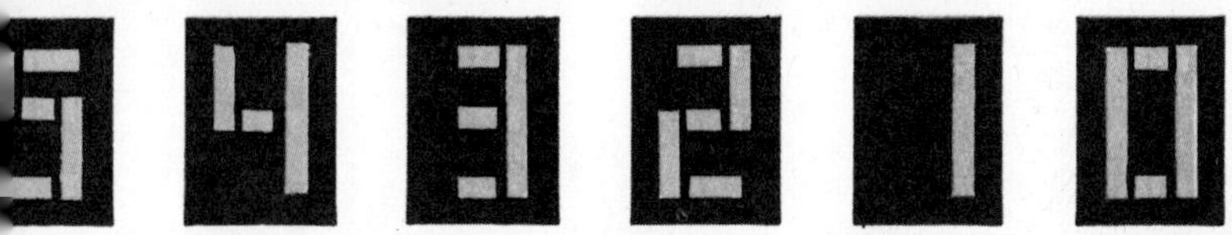

WHITMAN PUBLISHING COMPANY
RACINE, WISCONSIN

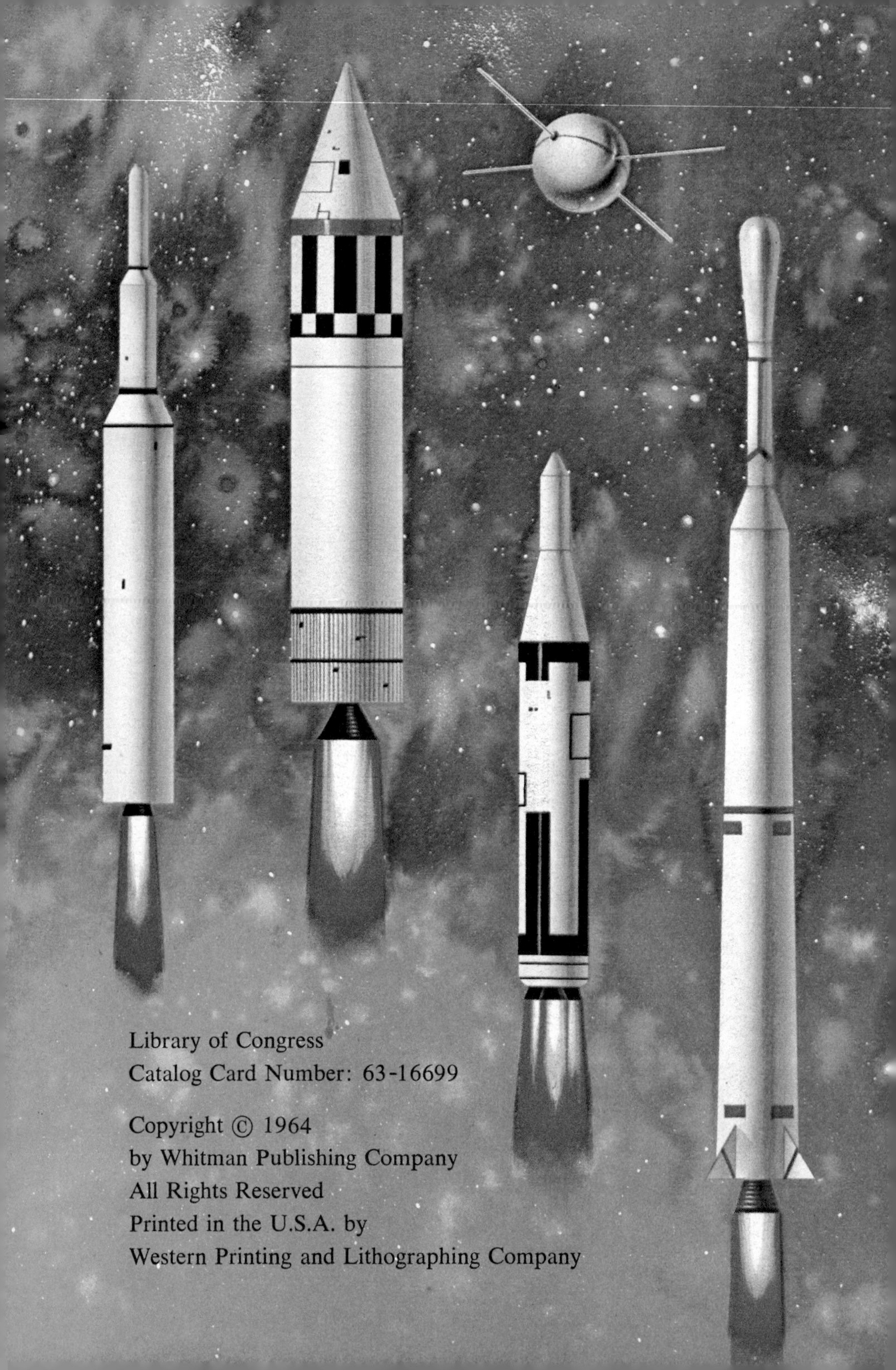

Library of Congress
Catalog Card Number: 63-16699

Printed in the U.S.A. by
Western Printing and Lithographing Company

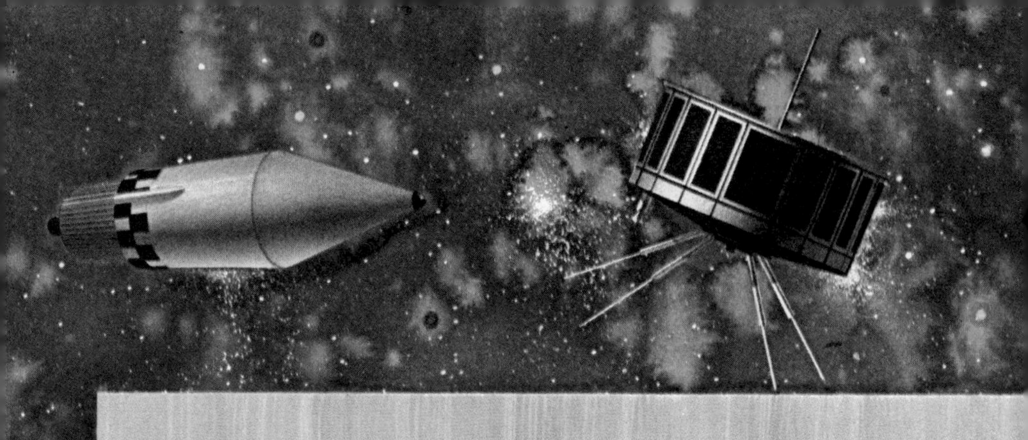

CONTENTS

Space Travel And You

SOMEDAY SOON you will click on your TV set and sit back to watch a colorful festival in Spain or a clown in a London music hall. These "live" programs will be sent to America by reflecting the radio waves from orbiting television satellites.

These and other wonders will be part of the new age of astronautics. *Astronautics* is a brand-new word and means the science of traveling through outer space. It is the science which will allow us to explore other worlds. It will affect all of our lives and be one of the great industries of the future.

Today's boys and girls will live and work in this exciting and adventurous new age. Many of the readers of this book will be astronautical engineers. Others will be the draftsmen and the mechanics who will help design and build the great spaceships of tomorrow.

The wonderful story of astronautics cannot be told in one book, or even ten books. The many parts of this new science of space flight rely on almost every field of knowledge. It is made up of important ideas from astronomy, mathematics, electronics, chemistry, physics, biology, nuclear engineering, and medicine—to name but a few! This book tells the story of only one small part of the science. But it is the most important part of all. It is the unfinished story of rocket power for space flight.

The start of the space age really began with the bellowing thunder of powerful rocket engines. These rocket engines were first used to power missiles and airplanes. Someday they will be used to power spaceships to far parts of the universe. But for a long time to come, space exploration will be confined to our own neighborhood in space—the solar system.

As a first step in understanding astronautics, let's learn some important things about Earth, the planets, and outer space. After all, *you* may be the first astronaut to set foot on the red sands of Mars!

Across Vast Distances To Whirling Worlds

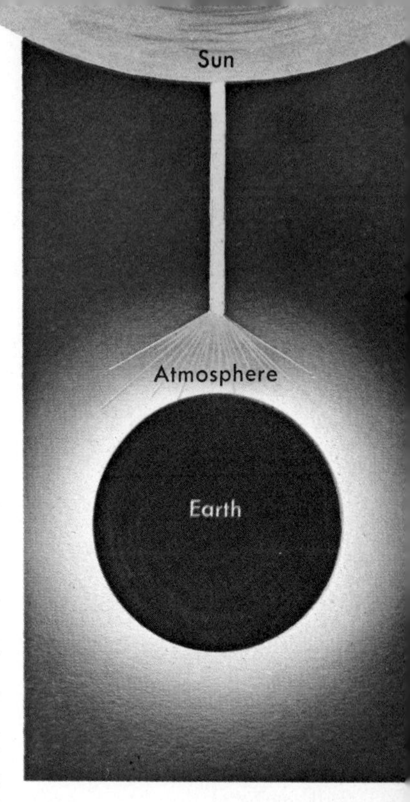

The sun's direct rays could easily burn the surface of the Earth. But Earth's atmosphere scatters the heat—and light—over a wide area.

OUR PLANET EARTH seems very large to us. In terms of space, however, it is only a grain of sand. We live on a ball of rock about eight thousand miles in diameter. It is revolving about the sun, spinning as it goes. A thin 120-mile-high layer of air protects us from the burning rays of the sun. Our atmosphere also contains life-giving oxygen for breathing.

The sun is the hub, the center, of the solar system and is the largest of the bodies. It is 865,000 miles in diameter, almost ten thousand times greater than the Earth. Astronomers have found nine major planets which circle around the sun. Each planet swings around the sun in its own oval-shaped path or orbit. The orbits are different sizes, but they have the sun as a common center.

Closest to the sun are Mercury, Venus, Earth, and Mars.

The four smallest planets, they are located in that order from the sun. The next four, farther from the sun, are the giant planets Jupiter, Saturn, Uranus, and Neptune. The most distant is Pluto and little is known about it. All of the planets revolve about the sun in the same direction. Like the Earth, they all spin as they move about the sun.

The distances between the planets are so great that they are hard to imagine. For example, the Earth is 93 million miles from the sun. This figure is so large that it is meaningless to our minds. It is important to find a way to compare and appreciate these vast distances. Because they are so great, spaceships will have to travel for long periods of time—even with the greatest possible speeds.

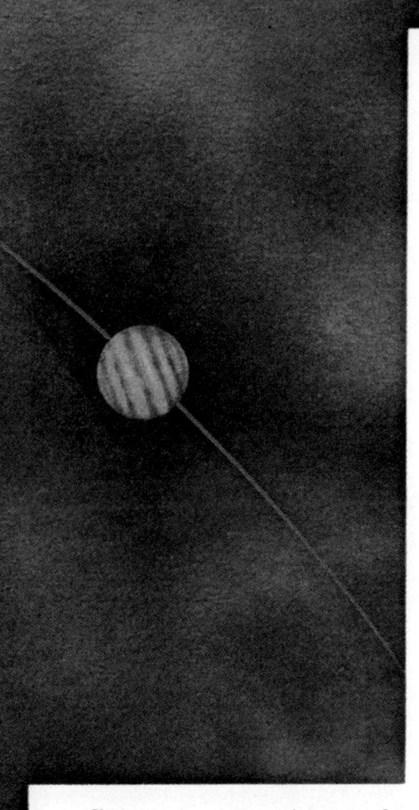

Can you imagine the Earth reduced to one millionth its size, or forty feet in diameter? The moon would be only ten feet across and a quarter of a mile away. A man would be invisible on the surface of the Earth. The sun would be ninety-three miles from our forty-foot Earth and a mile in diameter! The farthest planet, Pluto, would be only twenty feet across but would still be 3,600 miles from our forty-foot Earth!

Space is something of a junkyard, cluttered with pieces of rock and metal called meteorites. The Earth is continually bombarded with these particles from outer space. Most of them are burned up in the upper atmosphere by air friction. Protection from them will be one of the problems of spaceship design.

Great distances and speeding meteorite "bullets" are only two of the problems of astronautics. Its most dangerous enemies are the invisible pull of gravity and the emptiness of space!

Empty Space And Invisible Forces

THE ATMOSPHERE of the Earth does not come to a sudden stop 120 miles above us. Instead it becomes thinner and thinner until it trails off into the emptiness of space. At two hundred miles the air is so thin that we can say that space begins. Three-quarters of our life-giving oxygen is found in the first seven miles above the Earth. The lack of oxygen in space is a great enemy of space travel.

Jet airplanes in flight use the oxygen in air to burn the fuel in their powerful engines. They also need the atmosphere to provide the lifting force on their wings. Air-breathing engines and airplanes could never fly in the emptiness of space.

Spaceships, however, can travel through space—if they are given engines which do not depend upon oxygen in the atmosphere for combustion. In addition, the spaceships must carry enough oxygen for their crew for an entire journey.

But it is the invisible and ever-present grip of gravity that is the greatest enemy of all to space flight. The Earth attracts all objects around it; it tries to pull them to its surface. In fact, the Earth acts like a giant magnet attracting small iron particles to its surface. The Earth's gravity, however, is not due to magnetism. In fact we do not know exactly what causes it! But we do know how it acts.

The attracting force of gravity between two bodies depends upon their distance from each other, and their size. The greater the distance, the less they attract each other. Also, the larger body exerts a greater pull than the smaller one. If one is much greater than the other, all of the attracting is done by the larger of the two. A person is so small compared to the planet Earth

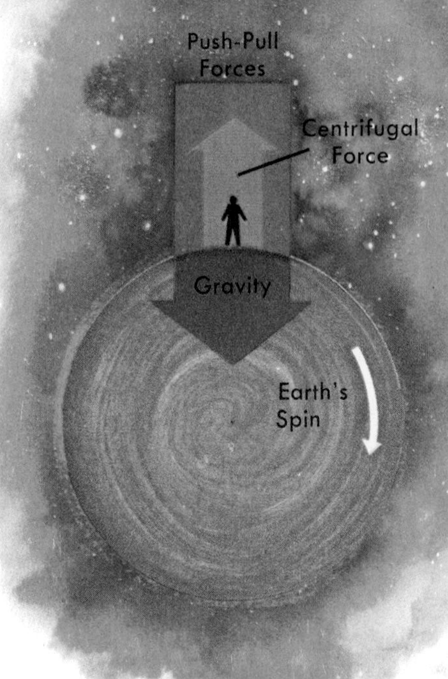

The Earth's spin causes things to be pushed away from its surface. The force is called centrifugal force. Gravity pulls all things toward Earth's center.

The pull of gravity is like the pull of a magnet on iron.

that the Earth does all of the pulling.

This mysterious attraction by the Earth is the cause of what we know as *weight*. Both weight and falling are due to gravity. As an object moves away from the Earth the force of gravity becomes weaker. Another way of saying this is that things "weigh less" far from the Earth. At four thousand miles the pull of gravity is only one fourth as strong as at the Earth's surface. A man weighing two hundred pounds on Earth would "weigh" only fifty pounds at four thousand miles.

Every planet in the solar system has a grasping field of gravity. The moon exerts a pull only one fifth that of the Earth. Larger planets have stronger forces of gravity. The mightiest of all is that of the sun—almost thirty times stronger than the Earth's. Because these forces can be felt over great regions of space, they are called *gravitational force fields*.

All space expeditions will start from the Earth's surface. It is then that the space rocket must do a task that is close to impossible. It must fight upward through and escape the downward pull of the Earth's field of gravity. The ship must carry its own energy as well as the weight of crew and equipment. Only by winning this battle, can we cruise to the planets in the soundless empty oceans of outer space.

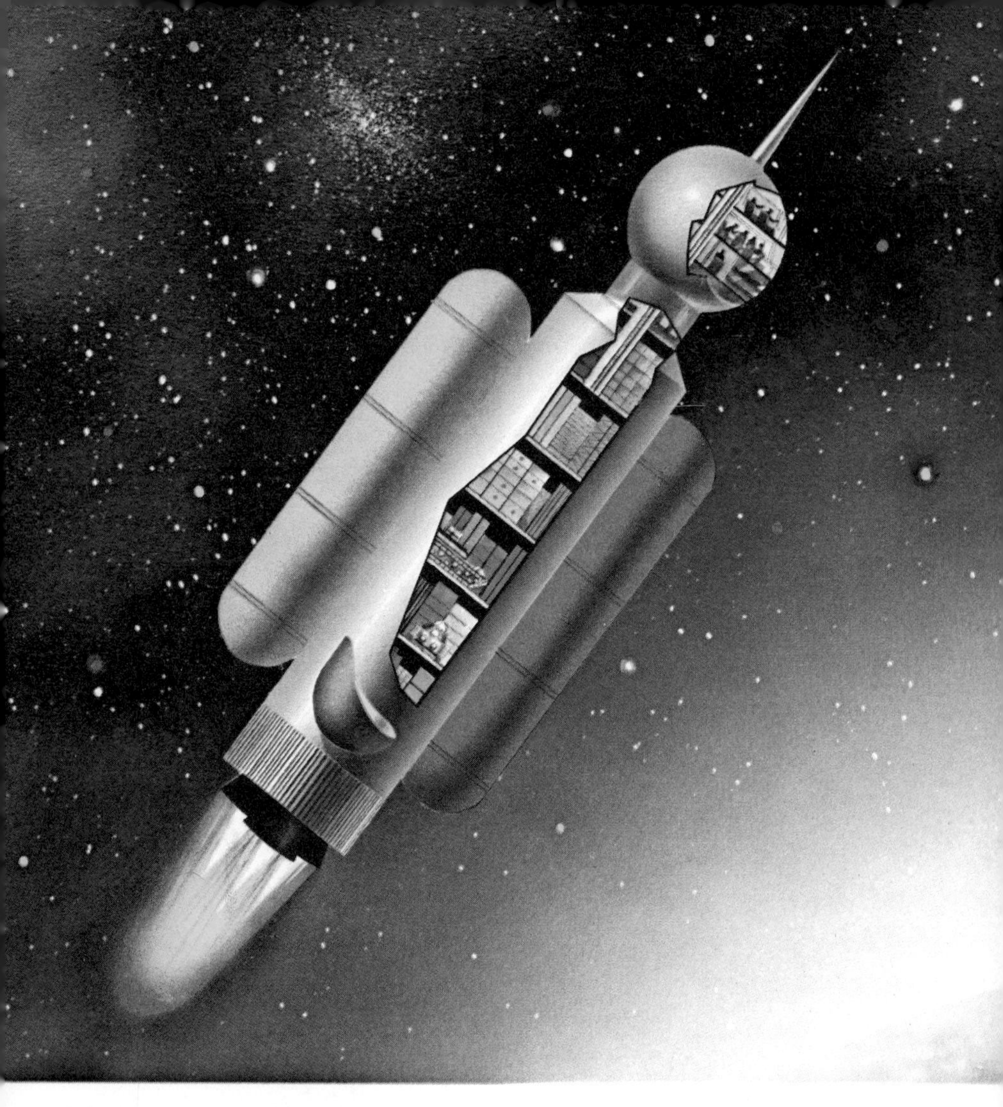

It is an astronautical fact that:

—only the rocket engine is powerful enough to escape the grip of Earth's gravity.

—only the rocket engine can operate in the vacuum of outer space.

—spaceships must obey the laws of space flight, the Laws of Motion. These were discovered more than three hundred years ago!

—spaceships will have to carry an oxygen supply along with their other supplies, for there is only emptiness in space.

—to cross the vast distances between the planets, spaceships will travel for weeks, months—even years.

Newton, Bicycles, And Rockets

ROCKETS ARE NOT new. The Chinese used them to defeat the Mongol invaders in 1232. These rockets were very small and made of black powder. Chinese writers called them arrows of fire.

Many men from many countries contributed to the science of rocketry. It is a fascinating story and would require a separate book to tell it. One man, however, made the greatest gift of all to space flight.

He was born in England in 1642 and probably never saw a rocket. Sir Isaac Newton, a space pioneer, left the world his famous Laws of Motion. The motion of anything, a planet, a train, or even a football, must obey these unchanging laws of nature.

The laws of nature are also the laws of space flight. A rocket engine's thrust and a spaceship's speed are governed by Newton's Three Laws of Motion.

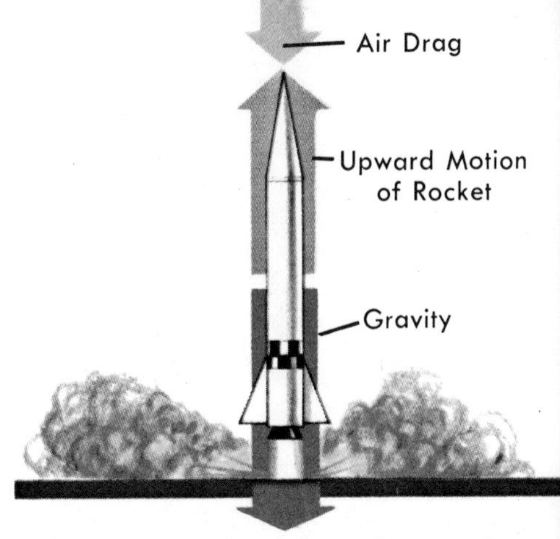

Gravity pulls the rocket downward. Air drag pushes against it. Rocket fuel provides power to overcome these.

Newton's First Law tells us that an object will always remain still, motionless—unless acted upon by an unbalanced force. It tells us that a moving object will continue to move at the same speed—unless acted upon by an unbalanced force.

This law applies to bicycles as well as rockets. Your bike remains still until you apply an unbalanced force by pushing it or stepping on the pedals. Also it always slows down and finally stops when you stop pedaling. That's because the unbalanced forces of air drag and tire friction have acted on it. When pedaling along at a steady speed, you are producing just enough force to overcome air drag and tire friction. There is no unbalanced force to slow you down and your speed does not change.

A rocket can coast forever in the emptiness of space. Far from the Earth there are only very weak gravitational

Next time you ride your bicycle, think of this: Your movement is governed by Newton's First Law, the same law that governs the movement of rockets. Air pushes against you, slowing you down. Your tires rub against the pavement, and this also slows you down. But by your pedaling you produce just enough force to exactly balance the air drag and tire friction.

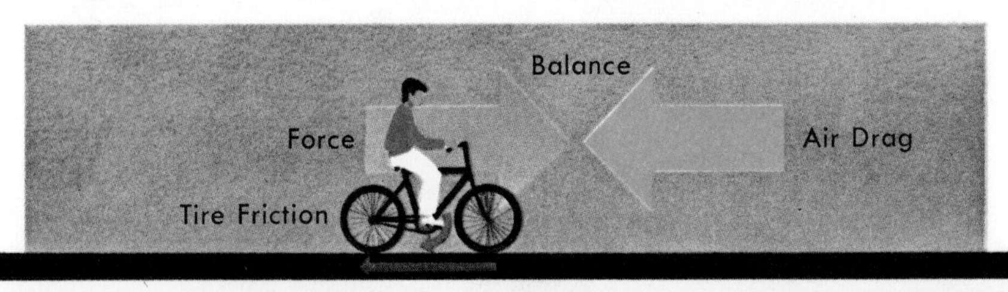

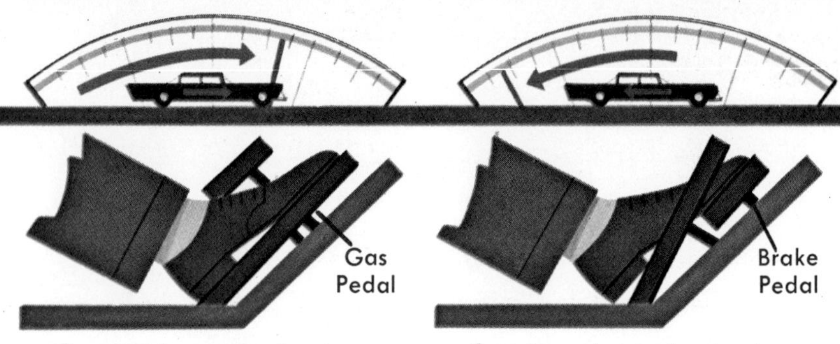

Car speeds up, accelerates. Car slows down, decelerates.

forces or air drag to change its speed.

Newton's Second Law explains how moving objects are made to speed up or slow down. It states that an unbalanced force acting on an object will change its speed. If a rocket is moving faster and faster each second, in the language of engineering it is *accelerating*. If its speed is becoming less each second, it is *decelerating*.

You can remember it this way. Pushing down on the gas pedal of a car makes the car accelerate. Pushing down on the brake pedal makes it decelerate.

Newton's Second Law also tells us another important fact about the top speed of rockets and bicycles. For the same unbalanced pushing force, a light object will accelerate faster than a heavier one.

Carrying a friend on the handlebars of your bicycle is a good example of Newton's Second Law. If you measure your top speed and the time needed to reach it with and without your friend, you will find that Mr. Newton was indeed right.

Reaction Force Action Force

The explosion inside a rifle hurls the bullet forward. At the same time there is an opposite reaction force. If you were holding this gun, you would feel the reaction force against your shoulder.

Newton's Third Law is sometimes the hardest to understand. It states that every action force always causes an equal and opposite reaction force. The firing of a rifle demonstrates the third law. The force of the explosion sends the bullet speeding out the barrel. This action force is matched by an equal and opposite reaction force, or thrust. The rifle recoils, or pushes back, against your shoulder.

A rocket engine shoots out a steady stream of "bullets" or gas particles in its exhaust jet. This is what causes the steady thrust force. The exhaust jet speed is the important thing in producing thrust. The faster the jet, the greater will be the thrust. Both the action and reaction forces occur inside the engine. This is why the thrust does not depend upon anything outside of the engine. Because of this it can operate in the vacuum of space.

When a towering space rocket—engines blazing—soars aloft, it follows a path laid out by Isaac Newton!

The action of a rocket is like the action of a bullet. Burning fuel inside the engine hurls a powerful stream of gas out of the rocket. At the same time there is an opposite reaction force, which pushes the rocket forward away from the gas. This opposite reaction force is called *thrust*.

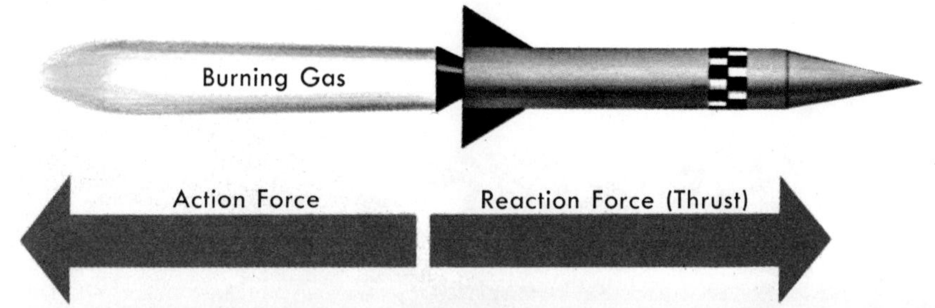

Spaceships And Cannonballs

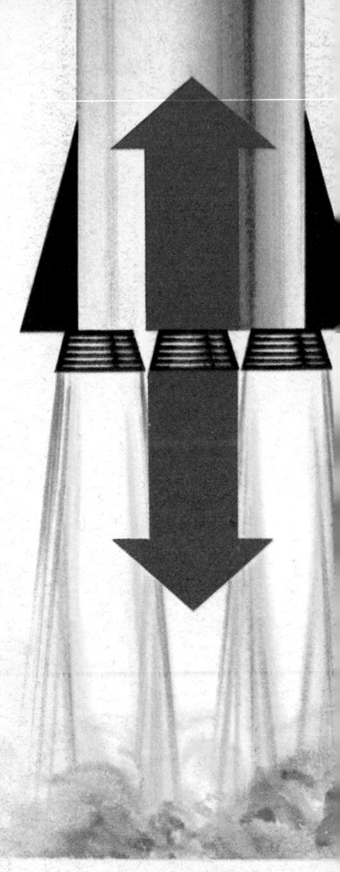

CANNONS and spaceships have one thing in common! They both hurl things out at great speeds. When a cannon fires, the shell flies out of the barrel. At the same time the gun leaps backward. The shell is pushed forward by the action force of the explosion. The cannon is thrust backward by the reaction force. Since the gun is heavier than the shell it does not move as fast or as far.

Two very important things determine the design of a space rocket: thrust and weight. They are best understood by putting wheels on a cannon.

Imagine a cannon mounted on a cart with wheels. The cart carries a pile of cannonballs and a man to fire them. Firing the cannon produces a thrust force and moves the cart in the opposite direction. Each shot will increase the speed just a little bit. Firing the cannon fast will make the cart accelerate rapidly backward.

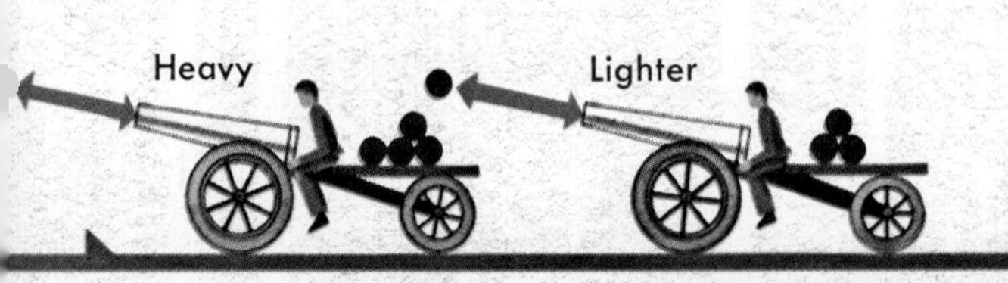

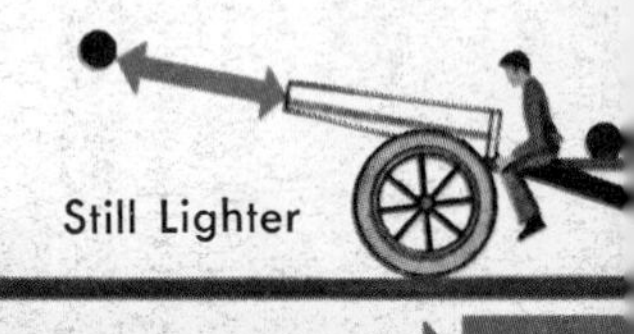

As cannonballs are fired, the cart will become lighter. Its speed will increase as it weighs less and less. The last cannonballs fired will increase the cart's speed more than those fired at the start. The cart's speed will be greatest when all the cannonballs have been fired.

Spaceships also reach their greatest speed after all the rocket propellant is burned. The ideas which apply to the cart and cannon also work for a spaceship. The cannon compares to the rocket engine, the cannonballs to the propellant, and the cart to the structure of a spaceship. The cannoneer represents the crew. The final or burnout speed of a spaceship depends greatly on the speed of its exhaust jet. Doubling the exhaust speed will make it travel twice as fast at burnout.

But there is also something else which determines the top speed of a rocket ship.

The cart's top speed depends upon the weight of the cart and the weight of the cannonballs it carried. The problem is a complicated one. Nevertheless it has been worked out

Like the cart which moves faster as it weighs less, so the rocket moves faster and farther as it uses its fuel supply.

mathematically by rocket engineers. The answer tells us to start with the greatest weight of cannonballs and the smallest possible weight of cart, cannon, and cannoneer. A spaceship then should carry the most propellant for the least weight of structure, rocket engine, and crew.

This is one of the greatest problems in astronautics. A small space rocket, about the size of the Atlas, would weigh one hundred tons just before launching. The exhaust jets would rush out at 5,500 miles per hour! If sixty-three tons of the rocket's weight were fuel, it would reach a burnout speed equal to its exhaust speed—or 5,500 miles per hour. See Rocket Number 1, page 25.

Good engineers, however, could easily design the rocket to carry eighty-seven tons of fuel and still weigh only one hundred tons. Its burnout speed would then be eleven thousand miles per hour—twice the exhaust jet speed. See Rocket Number 2, page 25.

A good engineer is never satisfied with what he builds. He always tries to improve it. Let's redesign our one-hundred-ton spaceship and throw out everything that we can—except the crew! Also let's make every part as light as possible—the engines, the hull, the tanks. In fact, let's put the propellant right in the hull and make the crew squeeze into midget quarters at the front!

Results? When we "fill 'er up," ninety-five tons of propellant go in and the ship still weighs only one hundred tons in all.

The fire switch is hit and the giant ship rises slowly from the launching pad. The reaction force from the thundering, fiery jets thrusts it aloft. This is the unbalanced force which makes the ship accelerate—even against the pull of gravity. As the ship rises, propellant is used and it becomes lighter. Thus the speed continues to increase.

Suddenly the shimmering jets vanish!

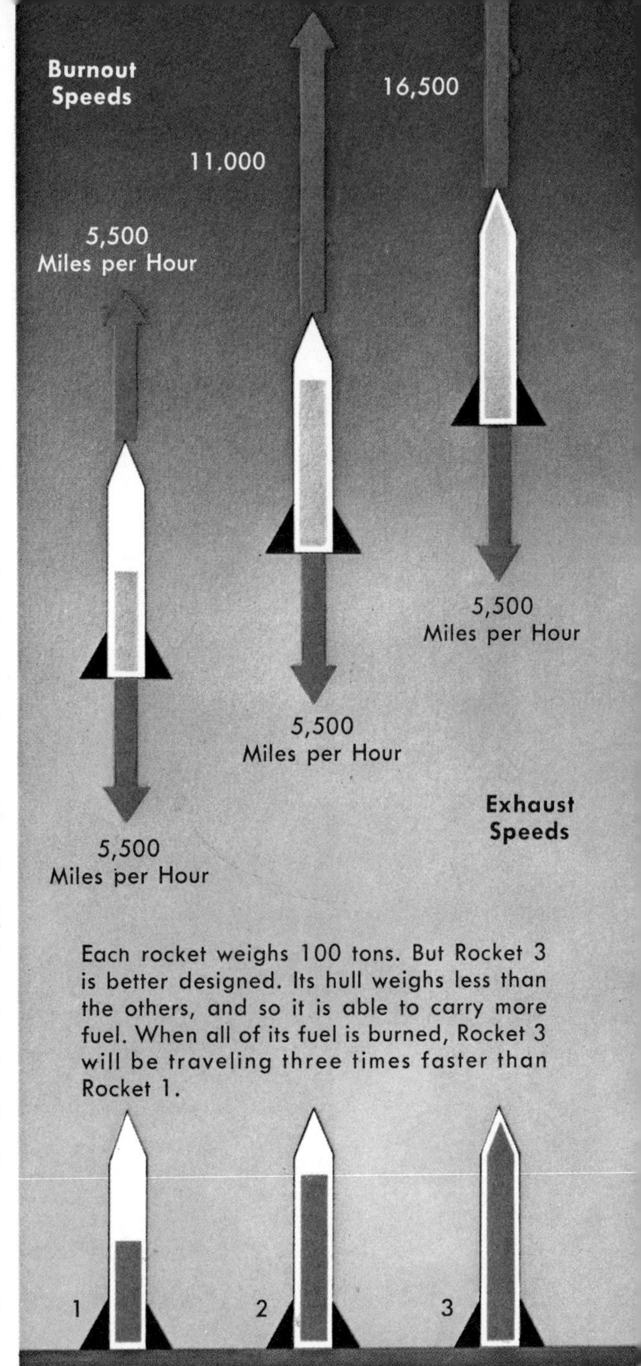

Each rocket weighs 100 tons. But Rocket 3 is better designed. Its hull weighs less than the others, and so it is able to carry more fuel. When all of its fuel is burned, Rocket 3 will be traveling three times faster than Rocket 1.

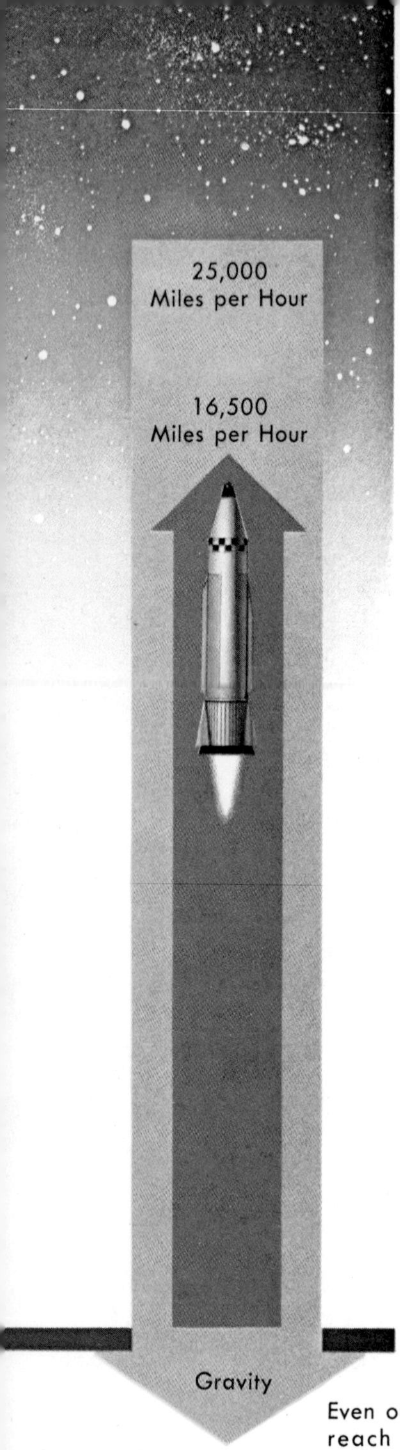

25,000
Miles per Hour

16,500
Miles per Hour

Gravity

The big engines have stopped; the propellant tanks are empty. The stripped-down ship is hurtling through space at 16,500 miles per hour. By squeezing in only seven tons more of propellant, and keeping the same launch weight, the burnout speed has been increased to *three* times the jet speed. See Rocket Number 3, page 25.

Modern rockets such as the Thor and the Atlas do almost this well. But unfortunately it is not good enough for space flight. To escape the gravitational grip of the Earth, a space rocket must reach a burnout speed of 25,000 miles per hour.

But how can we obtain an increase of 8,500 miles per hour at burnout? Trying to reduce the weight even more is not the answer. We can't throw out the crew and make the hull of balsa wood! Perhaps we could somehow increase the exhaust speed of the rocket engines? To answer that, we must learn about rocket engines.

Even our best rockets do not reach a speed of 25,000 miles per hour, needed to escape the pull of gravity.

Thrust, Energy, And "ISP"

THE ROCKET engines which lift our missiles and space probes away from the earth are marvels of modern engineering. They are the most powerful heat engines yet invented. A thrust force of 150,000 pounds is developed in an engine the size of a barrel!

To produce thrust, two things are needed: a propellant to shoot out, and some means of forcing it out at the greatest possible speed. The various kinds of rocket engines accomplish these two things in different ways. Energy must somehow be added to the propellant to produce a high exhaust speed. The oldest and most familiar energy source is the heat produced from combustion, or burning. Combustion powers our present-day rocket ships. Other forms such as nuclear, solar, and electrical energy can and will be used in powering spaceships in the future.

For a long time to come, however, spaceships will be

launched from the surface of Earth with engines using the heat energy of combustion. These are called "chemical" rocket engines because they rely on the energy stored by nature in the molecules of different chemicals. Chemical rockets produce thrust by burning two chemicals and then hurling them out at high speed. Just as a car burns air and gasoline, a chemical rocket engine burns an oxidizer and fuel. In the case of a car the oxygen in the air is the key which unlocks the stored chemical energy in the gasoline.

Combustion always requires a key in the form of an oxidizer to release the energy locked in the fuel. Both the oxidizer and fuel

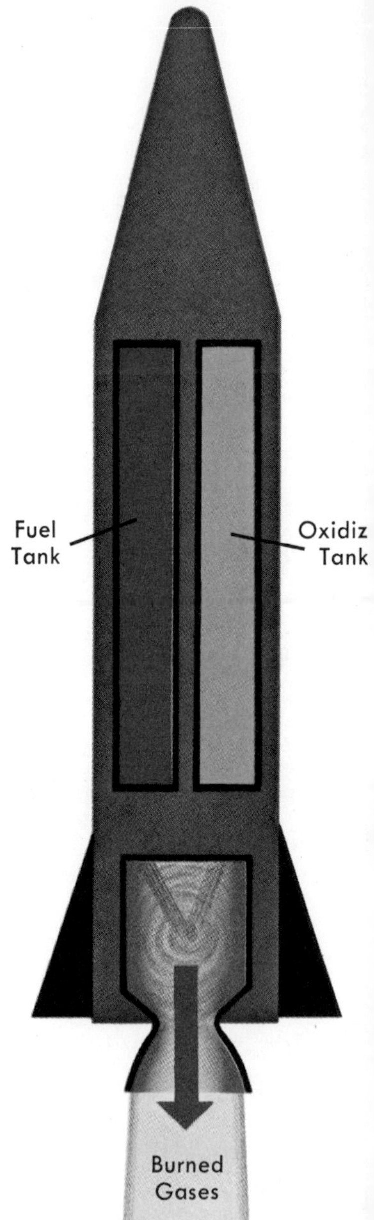

All rocket fuels and oxidizers have one thing in common: DANGER The best performers are always active chemicals. This means that they burn easily, or are poisonous or corrosive. Often they are all three Some fuel and oxidizer combinations begin to burn just on contac with each other.

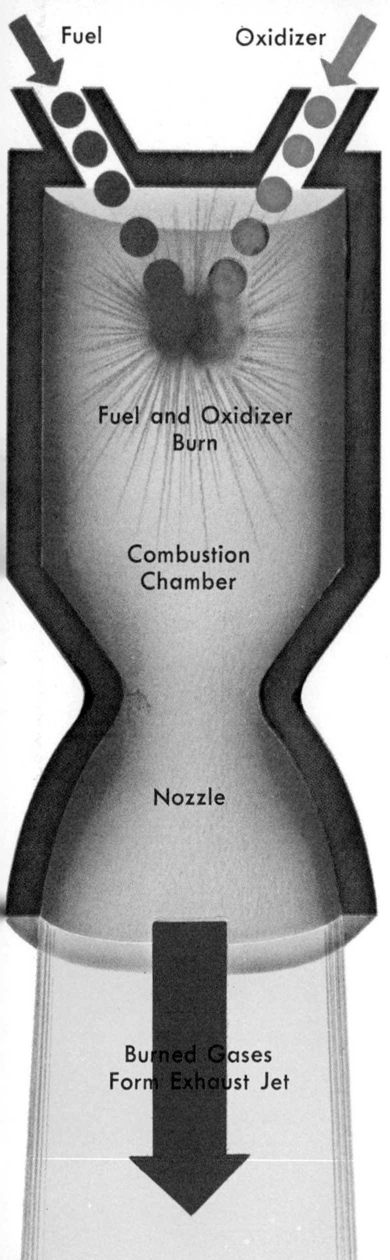

Red fuming nitric acid is a widely used rocket oxidizer. Rocket engineers use just the initials RFNA and call it *rifna*. RFNA can be used to burn ammonia as a fuel at a temperature of 4,200° F. Some missiles use RFNA to burn kerosene, and the flame temperature is 5,000° F.

are propellants, since it is their burned gases which are pushed out of the rocket. In the emptiness of outer space both the oxidizer and the fuel must be carried aboard the spaceship.

The performance of a rocket engine is no better than the chemical energy of its *propellant system*—the fuel to be burned and the oxidizer to burn it. The yardstick of engine performance is *exhaust jet speed,* and it springs only from the raging combustion of fuel and oxidizer. There are a number of chemicals which are good fuels, but there are only a few good oxidizers.

Rocket engineers have a way of comparing fuel and oxidizer combinations to decide which perform the best.

ISP

They call the performance *isp*. It means *specific impulse* and is written as ISP. The specific impulse is the amount of thrust produced from one pound of propellant in one second of engine operation.

To a rocket engineer, ISP means the same as "miles per gallon" does to a car owner. The larger the ISP, the smaller the amount of propellant needed to operate the engine. To the spaceship designer, it means a smaller propellant tank and a lighter, faster ship.

Low energy propellant systems produce as little as two hundred pounds of thrust from each pound of propellant burned. Present-day rocket engines use propellants which deliver about 250 pounds of thrust per pound burned. The high energy systems of the near future will deliver more than 350 pounds of thrust from each pound of propellant. But there is a roadblock ahead for chemical rockets. It is called the chemical energy limit.

The ISP is a handy way of expressing the greatest possible exhaust jet speed that a propellant system can produce. In fact, multiplying the ISP by twenty-two gives the jet speed in miles per hour. An ISP of three hundred means an exhaust jet speed of 6,600 miles per hour! Unfortunately, there seems to be a limit to the jet speeds that can be obtained by combustion. This is the result of Mother Nature's decision to limit the amount of energy

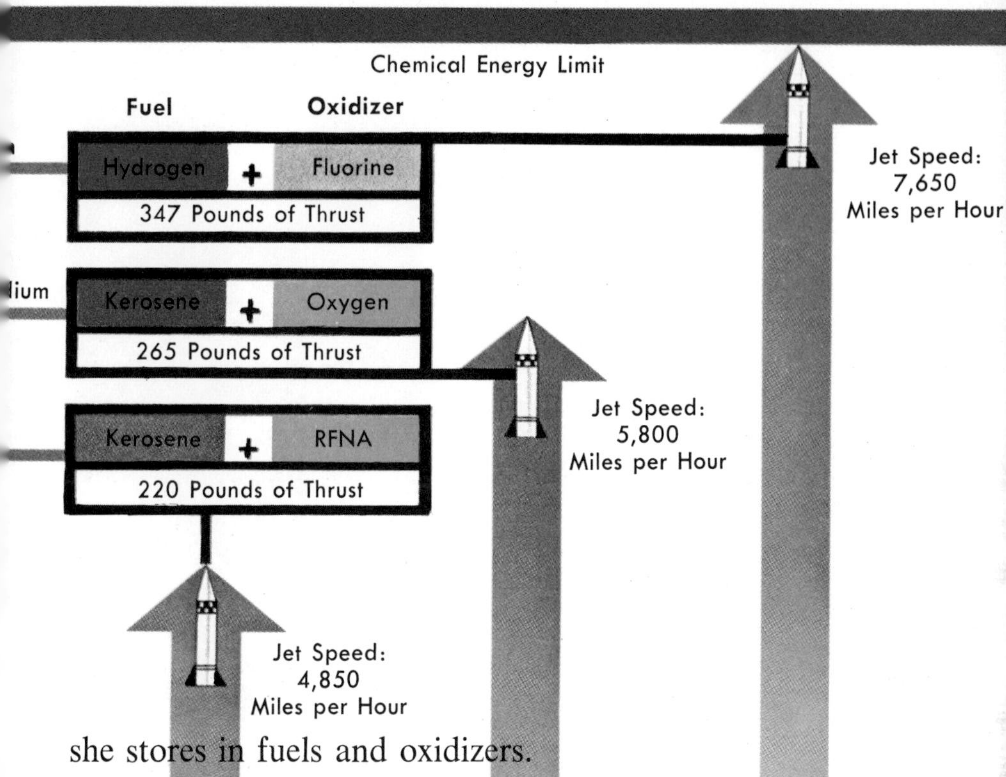

she stores in fuels and oxidizers.

The end of the road for chemical rockets is reached using deadly fluorine as the oxidizer to burn hydrogen as the fuel. This is the propellant system with the greatest possible performance and the worst possible behavior. Even the burned exhaust gases are poisonous. This villainous combination produces 347 pounds of thrust for each pound of propellant, with an exhaust jet speed of 7,650 miles per hour!

But the propellants are only the start. Rocket engines must be built to withstand the forces of a raging volcano. That is the next part of our story.

Thrust From Metal Volcanoes

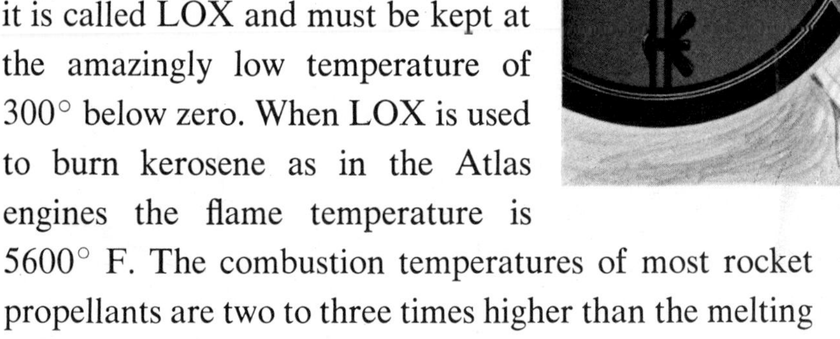

MOST OF TODAY'S large booster rocket engines use oxygen and kerosene as propellants. The oxygen carried in missile tanks has been cooled until it is no longer a gas but a liquid —liquid oxygen. In rocket language it is called LOX and must be kept at the amazingly low temperature of 300° below zero. When LOX is used to burn kerosene as in the Atlas engines the flame temperature is 5600° F. The combustion temperatures of most rocket propellants are two to three times higher than the melting point of steel!

One of the problems of building rocket engines is providing a furnace that can contain raging fires at high pressures. Any steel, for example, becomes as soft as rubber long before it actually melts. The furnace of a liquid propellant rocket engine is called the combustion chamber. A trick is required to keep the combustion chamber strong and lightweight. It is called *regenerative cooling.*

In regenerative cooling, one of the propellants, usually the fuel, is forced through narrow passages in the wall of the combustion chamber before it is burned. It acts as a coolant, keeping the walls of the combustion chamber far below the melting point of the metal. Sometimes a thin film of fuel is squirted along the inside wall. As it evaporates, it provides additional help in cooling the wall.

The carburetor of a car engine has the important job of mixing the right amounts of gasoline and air for best combustion. Liquid propellant rocket engines need a kind of a carburetor too. In addition the fuel and oxidizer must be carefully kept apart until the instant of combustion. These are the jobs of the *injector* which forms one end of the combustion chamber. The injector plate is a maze of small passages which feed hundreds of tiny injection holes. Through these, the many separate fuel and oxidizer streams rush into the combustion chamber.

The hourglass shape of the exhaust nozzle is the rocket engine's outstanding feature.

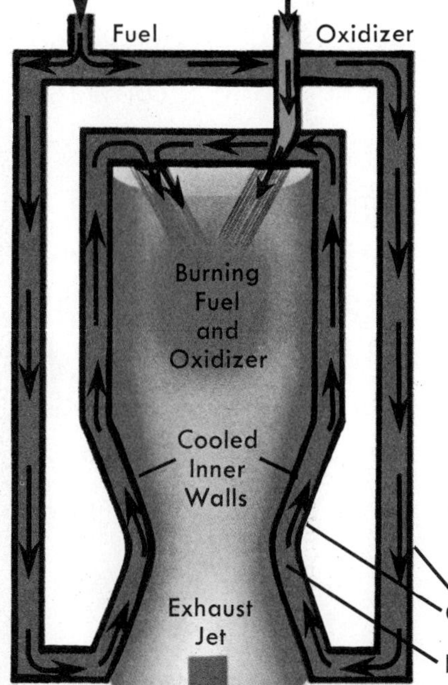

Fuel is pumped through the walls of the combustion chamber.

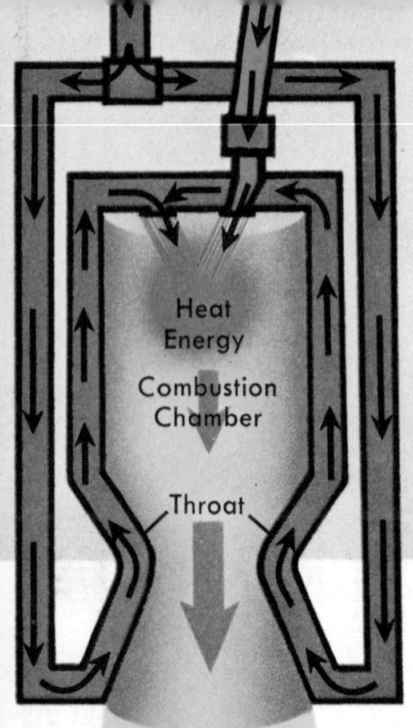

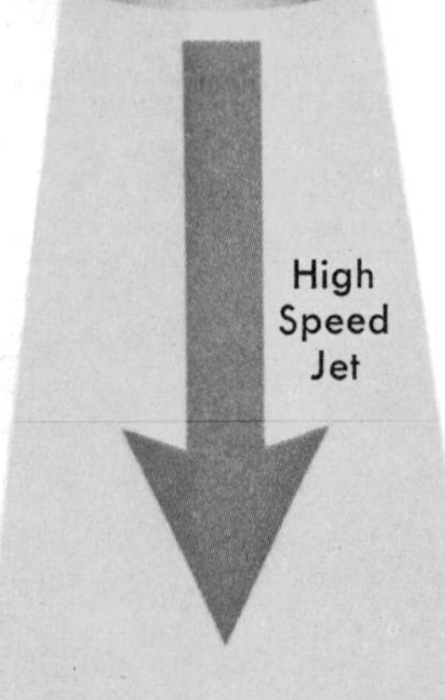

All rocket engine nozzles look pretty much alike. Starting from the combustion chamber, they squeeze together. At the smallest point, the throat, they again become larger. The nozzle has the task of changing heat energy into the moving energy of the high-speed exhaust jet.

The hot burned gases flowing into the squeezed down, converging, part of the nozzle find less and less room to pass through. They only escape by speeding up or accelerating. At the throat, the rushing gases reach exactly the speed of sound. As the gases pass through the throat into the widening part of the nozzle, they accelerate to speeds much greater than the speed of sound. Rocket nozzles must always narrow and then widen to accelerate the burned propellants to supersonic speeds.

The nozzle also requires cooling. Of all parts of the rocket engine, the metal walls at the throat receive the most heat. This is the most difficult place to cool.

Almost all liquid propellant engines are regeneratively cooled. This permits the construction of the nozzle and combustion chamber as a single unit. A great many lengths of small steel tubing are bent to shape and welded together. The hollow tubes are the regenerative cooling passages. The rocket engineer calls the combustion chamber and the exhaust nozzle assembly the *thrust chamber*.

Liquid propellant engines require pumps. The propellants are burned in the combustion chamber at thirty-five times the pressure of the air at the Earth's surface. Pumps are needed to draw the oxidizer and the fuel from their storage tanks and force them into the combustion chamber. Every engine must have an oxidizer pump and a fuel pump, and a means of powering them.

A liquid propellant engine needs other parts in addition to the turbopumps and thrust chamber. There must be some way to start and stop the engine, perhaps even to restart it in the emptiness of outer space.

Part of the job is done by propellant valves. Two are required: an oxidizer valve and a fuel valve. They

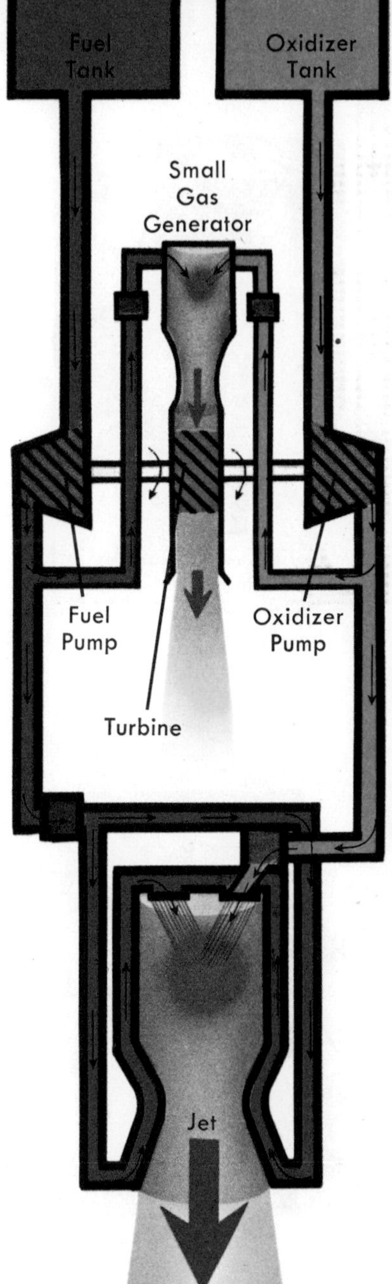

In today's rockets a small gas generator burns small amounts of the propellants. The small high-speed jet from the generator strikes a turbine wheel. This wheel drives the pumps which pull the propellants from their tanks to the engine.

Thrust Chamber Valve

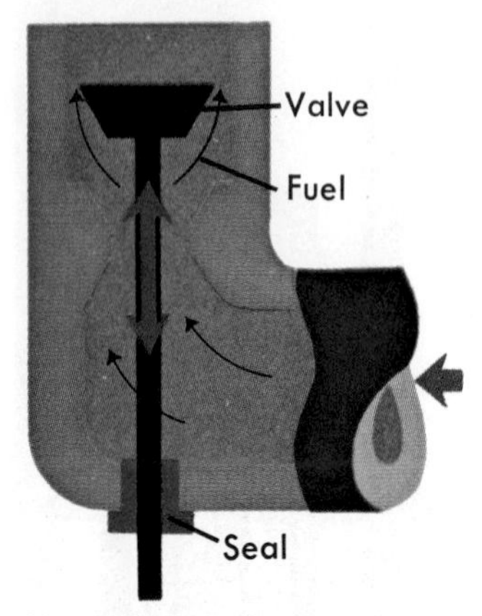

Here, fuel is flowing into the combustion chamber. When the valve closes, the flow of fuel is stopped and the engine stops.

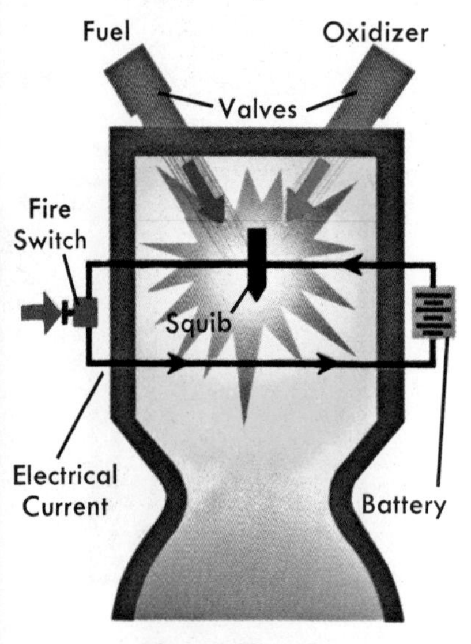

Thrust Chamber

To start the engine, a squib is ignited by an electric current at just the moment when the valves are opened.

control the flow of propellants into the thrust chamber. It is very important that they open and close quickly—and that they do not leak! They are called the thrust chamber valves.

The engine is stopped by closing the thrust chamber valves. Starting it, however, is not so simple. The propellants must be ignited—and at just the right instant after the valves open. This is done with a black powder squib something like a firecracker. It is ignited by an electrical current.

Sometimes the squib is a little slow in igniting the incoming propellants. By the time it does, there is too much in the thrust chamber. This is called a hard-start. It usually means, "The engine blew up!"

Another and quite different kind of chemical rocket engine is being used more and more in space research. This is the solid propellant rocket engine. It differs greatly from its relative the liquid propellant engine. In the liquid propellant engine the fuel and oxidizer are always carried in separate tanks which are part of a spaceship's structure. The solid propellant rocket stores *and* burns its propellant in one big tank. This is possible only because the propellant is in one solid chunk.

To form this solid chunk, the fuel and oxidizer chemicals are mixed with another called the binder. The result is a thick syrupy mixture almost like molasses. It is poured into a mold and heated gently. After several days, it hardens into a solid *grain*. The solid grain contains both the chemical energy and the propellant material for producing thrust. It is similar to a stick of dynamite. All of the chemicals are there in one place ready to explode.

The solid grain is slipped, or sometimes actually cast, into a lightweight metal cylinder. This is the combustion chamber *and* the tank. The grain is shaped in special ways so that it can burn on inside surfaces. The simplest

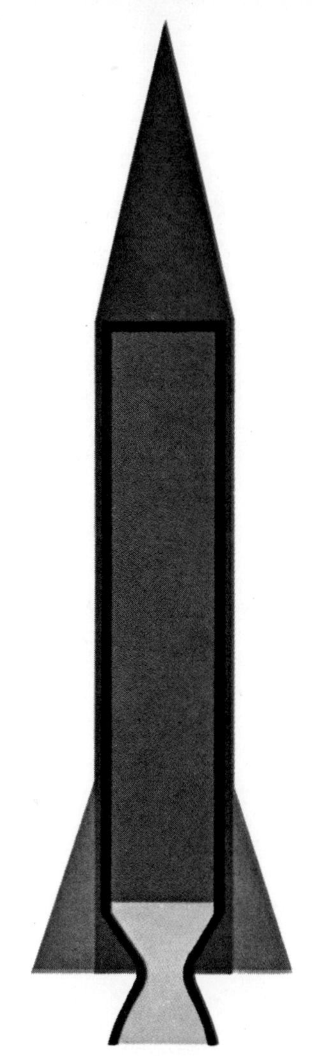

Solid Propellant Rocket

Solid propellant rockets store and burn their fuel in one big tank. The fuel, oxidizer, and a thickener called a *binder* are combined in a solid grain.

Fuel + Oxidizer + Binder = Solid Grain

grains are end burning, in the manner of a cigarette. Most commonly, however, there is a hole down the center. These are similar to a hollow log burning from the inside outward. The flame temperatures of solid propellants are very high. The grain itself protects the thin metal wall from the heat until the last few seconds of burning. The hot burned gases are speeded up by the narrowed exhaust nozzle, as with the liquid propellant engine.

Solid propellant engines are simpler mechanically than the liquid propellant type. They do not need separate tanks, pumps, valves, or other moving parts. They also carry all of their chemical energy right in the combustion chamber. However, this can be extremely dangerous. With the right conditions the entire grain can explode.

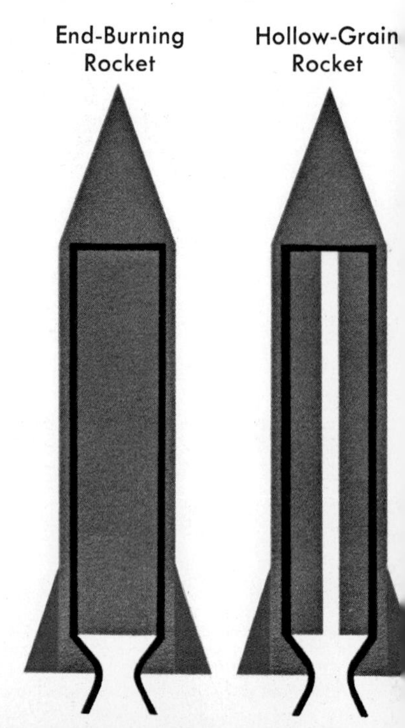

Solid propellant rockets seem simple. That is why they attract the interest of the amateur rocket builder. But they are not simple. There are important relationships between propellant chemistry, nozzle size, and grain shape. These must be exactly correct. If they are not, the rocket becomes a dangerous bomb.

Building and testing rockets is dangerous, even when done by a company with vast experience. It should never be tried by a home rocket builder, not even on the smallest scale.

Like any other, the solid propellant engine has certain disadvantages. Solid propellants have lower values of ISP than liquids. Solid grains sometimes crack, due to being dropped or to a sudden change in temperature. Even a tiny crack inside the grain will make the engine explode the instant it is started! In addition a solid propellant rocket engine cannot be stopped and then restarted in the vacuum of outer space.

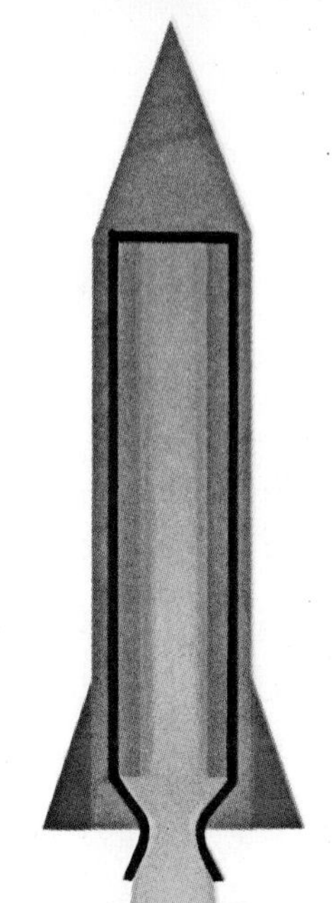

Solid propellant rockets are simpler than other kinds, since they carry all of their energy right in the combustion chamber.

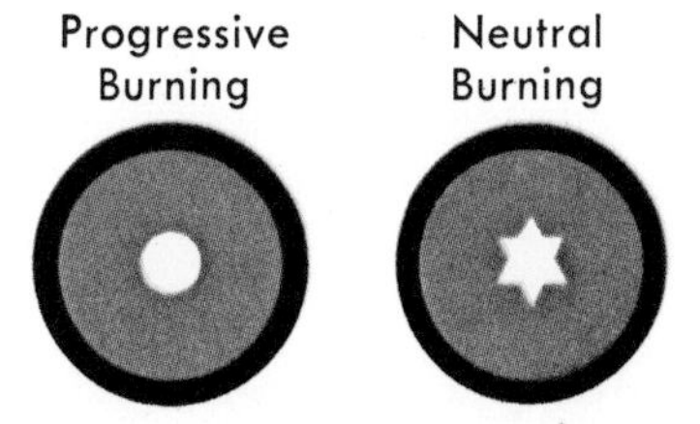

Thrust of solid propellant rockets can be controlled by the shape of the hole in the center. Thrust will increase as the grain with the round hole burns. Thrust from the grain with the star-shaped hole will remain fairly constant.

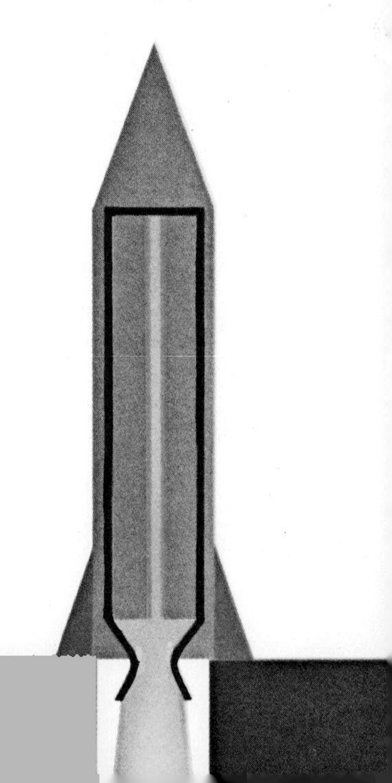

Escape Equals Rockets-On-Rockets

ESCAPING FROM THE EARTH! That's the first step and the giant step of space flight. Once free of the Earth's pull, a space rocket can coast to the planets. If Mars is the destination, the rocket must move along just the right path to meet the red planet. Remember that all three—Earth, the space rocket, and Mars—are moving. Finally, the ship must be able to land safely on the planet.

While the last two steps are difficult, they are easy compared to escaping Earth's gravity.

The task is something like climbing a steep hill on your bicycle. Suppose that the hill is at first very steep, but slowly rounds off to a flat level road at the top. By starting to pedal furiously ahead of time, you can often build up enough speed to coast over the top. But some hills are too steep and too high to do this. Then you coast part way and stop. Rather than roll back down, you hop off and walk your bike to the top.

And so it is with space rockets—except that when the "hill" is too high the crew cannot hop out and walk the ship to the top!

The only way a space rocket can escape the clutch of gravity is by building up enough speed to allow it to coast over the top of an imaginary gravitational hill. For the spaceship this amounts to a straight-up hill four thousand miles high! If the spaceship does not have enough speed it plunges back to Earth.

Scientists have long been able to calculate this important speed. For our planet Earth it is an incredible 25,000 miles per hour. If a rocket fails to reach this speed by even the tiniest amount, it will always be pulled back to Earth. This speed is important enough to be given a name—escape speed. Each planet has an escape speed which depends upon its size. For

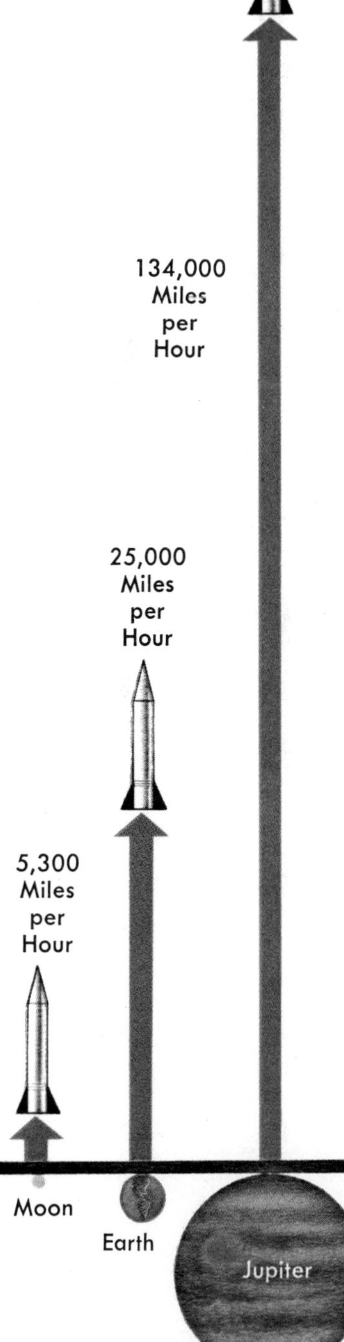

Gravity is like a steep hill. A rocket must build up enough speed to climb the hill and slide over the top. Each planet's gravity, and the rocket speed needed to escape it, is determined by the planet's size.

the moon it is a mere 5,300 miles per hour. For the giant Jupiter it is 134,000 miles per hour!

Mother Nature has not cooperated very well in helping the astronaut. First of all, she has limited the amount of heat energy that can be obtained from combustion. This means that even using the hottest propellant system known, hydrogen and fluorine, the rocket exhaust speed can be only eight thousand miles per hour.

Second, she insists that rocket ships reach a burnout speed of 25,000 miles per hour to break away. Of course the burnout speed also depends upon carrying the most propellant with the least weight of crew and ship. Then perhaps a "lean and light" rocket might do it? Let's see!

Remember our small rocket with a launch weight of one hundred tons? This was a very good design indeed. In fact it is about the best that can be done. Suppose this rocket carries ninety-five tons of propellant. That leaves only five tons for the total weight of rocket motors, controls, hull and structure, and the crew and their cabin.

But most importantly, this stripped-down spaceship at burnout would travel at three times the speed of its rocket exhaust. Using LOX and kerosene, this would be a respectable 16,500 miles per hour. However, that is far, far short of the 25,000 miles per hour necessary to break away from the Earth's field of gravity.

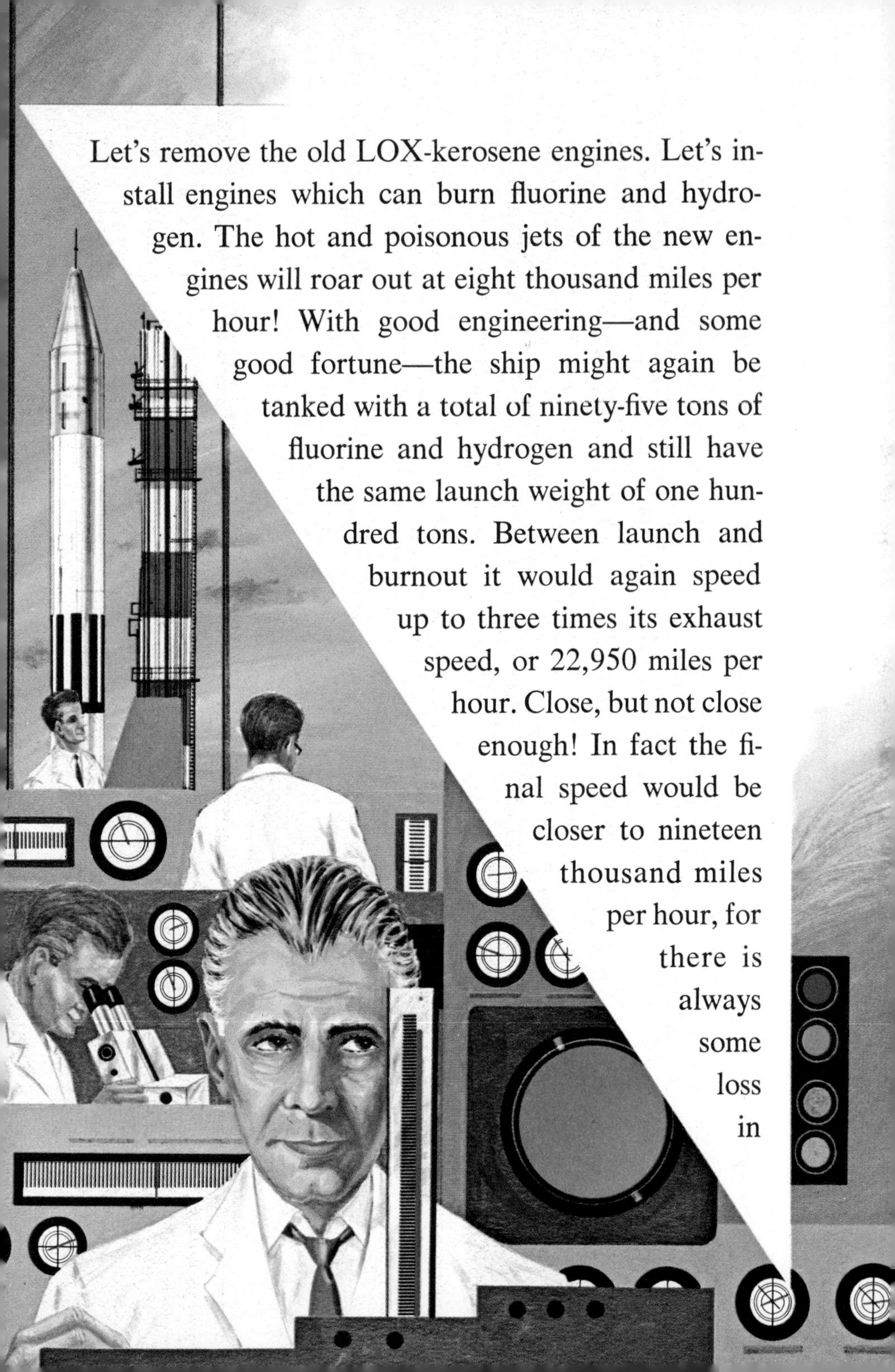

Let's remove the old LOX-kerosene engines. Let's install engines which can burn fluorine and hydrogen. The hot and poisonous jets of the new engines will roar out at eight thousand miles per hour! With good engineering—and some good fortune—the ship might again be tanked with a total of ninety-five tons of fluorine and hydrogen and still have the same launch weight of one hundred tons. Between launch and burnout it would again speed up to three times its exhaust speed, or 22,950 miles per hour. Close, but not close enough! In fact the final speed would be closer to nineteen thousand miles per hour, for there is always some loss in speed from "lingering" in the Earth's field of gravity.

The discouraging performance of this stripped-down and souped-up rocket points out one of the most important lessons in astronautics! *It is impossible to escape from the Earth with the best possible rocket using the energy of chemical combustion.*

But there is another way to speed up to 25,000 miles per hour and escape. It can be done with the *multistaged* rocket, a rocket carrying rockets. Using this idea, almost any burnout speed can be reached. It is the only means by which we can reach the planets. But Mother Nature is not an easy loser, and the price of victory is always high.

Multistaging rockets means using one rocket to carry another aloft. When the first stage or booster rocket is exhausted it falls away. The second-stage rocket ignites and adds to the speed and altitude obtained from the booster. The second-stage rocket can often gain extra speed

because of reduced air drag. Satellite-launching and space-probe rockets need three and sometimes four stages.

Mountain climbers use much the same scheme in conquering a mighty peak. A great number of men bring in the supplies to the base camp. Then perhaps only eight men carry supplies part way up to the first camp. Four men might struggle up with supplies to a higher second camp. Only two lightly loaded men make the final climb to the top.

Each additional rocket stage carries less weight but adds to the speed and height of the last. In fact, if each stage is designed to be equally efficient, it will double the burnout speed of the previous one. It would seem that there is no limit to the burnout speed obtainable by adding stages. But there is.

Suppose we engineer a two-stage rocket using our previous one hundred ton space "hot rod." If it is mounted on top of a first-stage booster of equally efficient design, the burnout speed will be doubled.

Of course the new booster rocket will be bigger. But how much bigger?

The new first-stage rocket must have a burnout weight of one hundred tons. To be as good a propellant container as its second stage "little brother," it must carry 1,900 tons of propellant. This means that the complete two-stage rocket would have a launch weight of two thousand tons! With a medium energy propellant system of LOX and kerosene, the final burnout speed would be about 26,200 miles per hour.

This is more than enough speed to escape the Earth. The extra one thousand miles per hour is just enough to permit the empty five-ton second stage to travel one way to Mars—in 260 days. The extra speed has been obtained by building a two-stage rocket *twenty* times heavier than the original. The first-stage booster rocket engines would have to deliver more than one million pounds thrust! If three stages were used, the total weight would be 400,000 tons—the weight of eight average ocean liners.

The cost of staging is size and weight. Every stage added multiplies the total weight

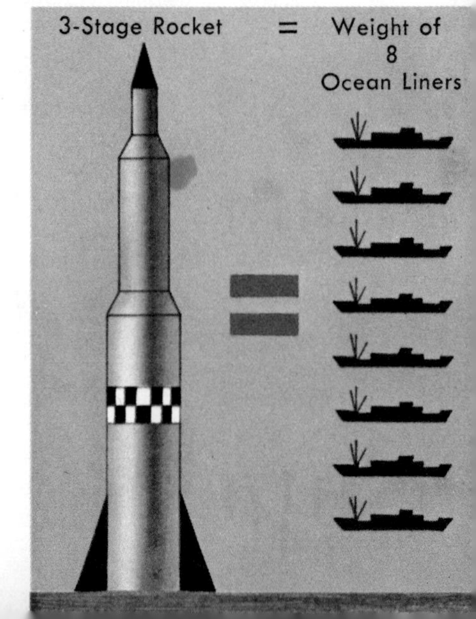

by twenty! In short, the price of speed is size, weight, and dollars.

Staging has other disadvantages. Each stage must be a complete rocket with its own pumps, tanks, engines, and controls. With three times as many parts, we have three times the chance of things going wrong. Also each stage must be connected to the next so that it can be separated by a radio signal. These interstage connections add extra weight to the rocket and they do not always work! Sometimes the burned-out stage "hangs up" or fails to separate from the others. This completely destroys the performance.

Adding more and more stages to reach the great speeds needed results in ships the size of skyscrapers. It is rather like using an empty ocean liner to carry a baseball! But there is one big difference: We know that ocean liner will always get there, but with a three- or four-stage rocket we are not so sure!

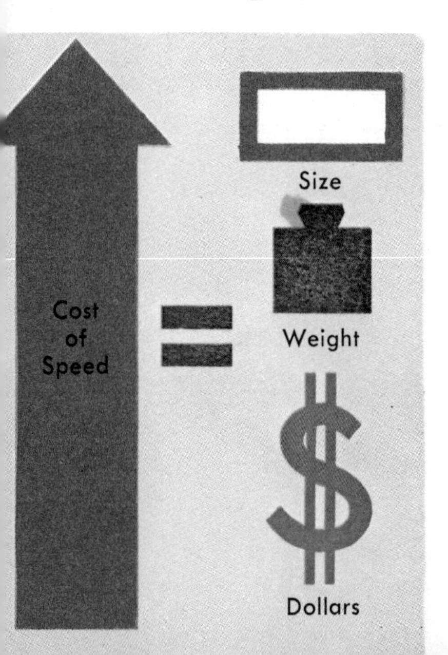

The entire future of space exploration hangs on finding a way to reduce the size of spaceships. Can this be done? To find the answer, let's look into the future!

Atoms, Ions, And The Future

A WEARY rocket engineer looking at the twisted remains of a bad shot defined astronautics. He called it the science of doing the impossible! What he meant was that there will always be more problems than answers. The most important of today's problems is reducing the size of spaceships.

Of the many ideas of many scientists and engineers, only two have survived. Perhaps you have already guessed that one of them uses the enormous energy locked in the atom—a nuclear rocket engine. The other, however, will be something of a surprise!

Everyone knows that an airplane cannot fly around the Earth without landing a number of times for fuel. The supersonic jet bombers of our Strategic Air Command do this quite regularly however! How? They are refueled in the air by "flying gas stations" or jet tankers. The very same idea can be used for space flight. It is called orbital refueling.

Over thirty years ago, an Austrian engineer suggested that tanker ships be used to refuel a single spaceship orbiting far above the Earth. A spaceship with a burnout speed of eighteen thousand miles per hour could be guided into a circular orbit 25,600 miles above the Earth. It could whirl around the Earth forever, held only by a feeble thread of gravity. With a little thrust, it could speed up seven thousand miles per hour and escape the Earth.

Special cargo rockets could make the Earth-to-orbit trip carrying propellant and supplies for interplanetary voyages. Eventually they would be flyable, designed to return safely to the Earth for another trip. The cargo rockets, of course, would have to reach a burnout speed of eighteen thousand miles per hour to enter the orbit of the spaceship. With bursts of thrust from small control rockets, the cargo rockets could position themselves alongside the spaceship and transfer supplies.

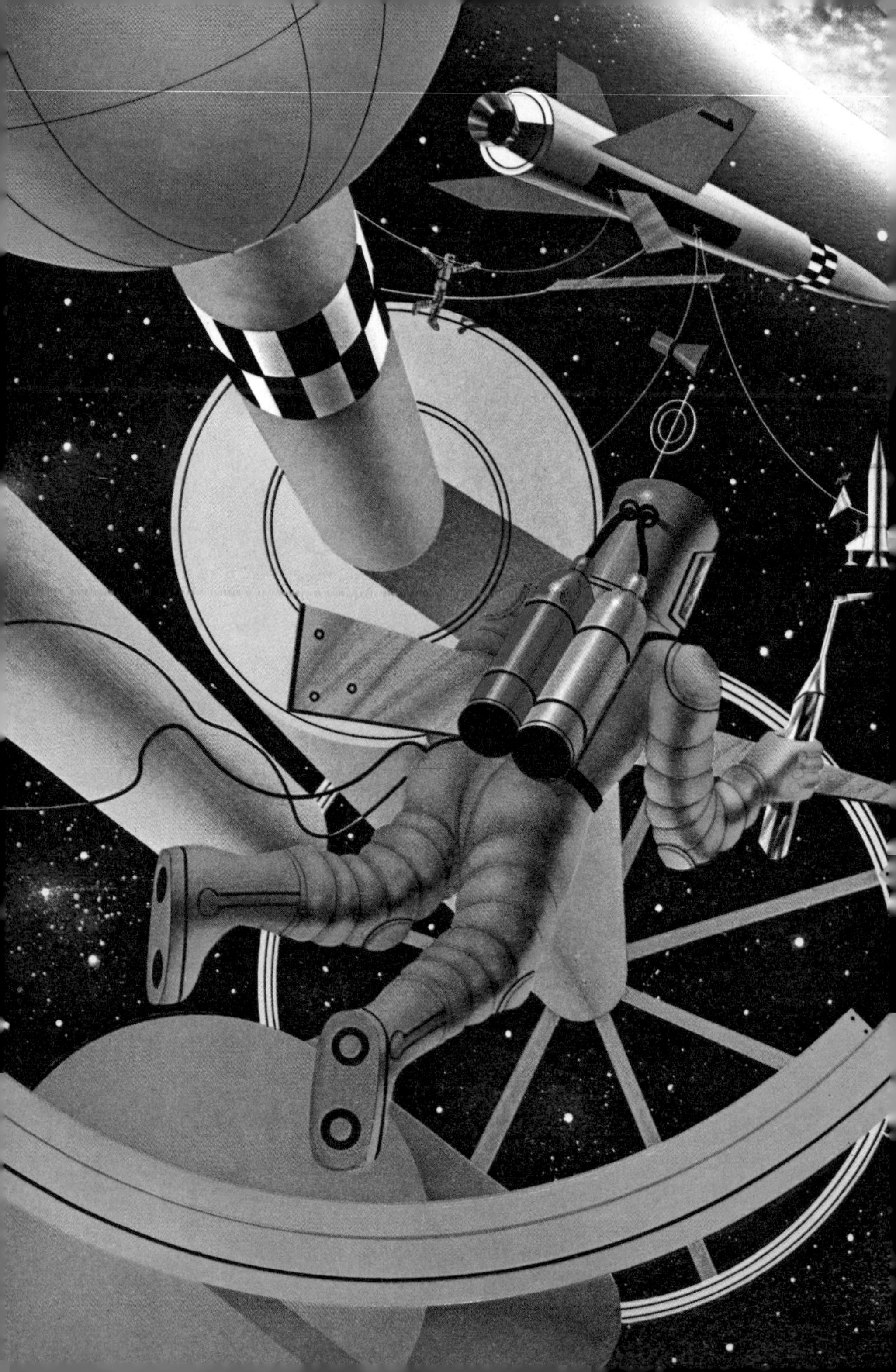

Even today astronautics is a great industry involving thousands of people and millions of dollars. A special branch of our government has the huge task of directing this effort. It is called the NASA—National Aeronautics and Space Administration. The brilliant engineers and scientists of the NASA are responsible for planning the research and development for the next step in space exploration.

They have made a very careful study of a manned expedition to Mars, starting from an orbit about the Earth. The plan consists of using cargo rockets to launch men, tools, supplies, and the parts of a special spaceship into a circular orbit far above the Earth. Using protective space suits, men will assemble the Mars ship in outer space. When finished, the interplanetary ship will be able to transport eight men to Mars. There will be supplies for a stay of several months. And of course there will be a carefully thought-out plan and supplies for the spaceship to make a safe return to the home orbit.

Surprisingly, the Mars expedition could be made using only the thrust of chemical rockets. It would require lifting a total of twelve hundred tons into orbit—and eleven hundred of the twelve hundred tons would be propellant for the Mars ship!

NUCLEAR ROCKET ENGINE

The Earth-to-orbit cargo ships for this giant moving job would weigh five hundred tons at launch. They would need a booster engine of 1½ million pounds thrust. Finally—one hundred *successful* trips would have to be made!

Orbital refueling does make manned space flight possible, even with the limited energy of chemical combustion. But it is possible only at great cost and effort. What can be done to reduce the risk and price of space flight?

The answer is the use of atomic energy for rocket propulsion. The number of ways in which it can be used to produce thrust is astonishing. There are two engines, however, which are particularly important. These are almost ready for flight testing. They have only one thing in common: Both use a nuclear reactor as an energy source. In every other way, they are completely different.

Smaller, more powerful spaceships will be possible using the nuclear fission rocket engine. The nuclear

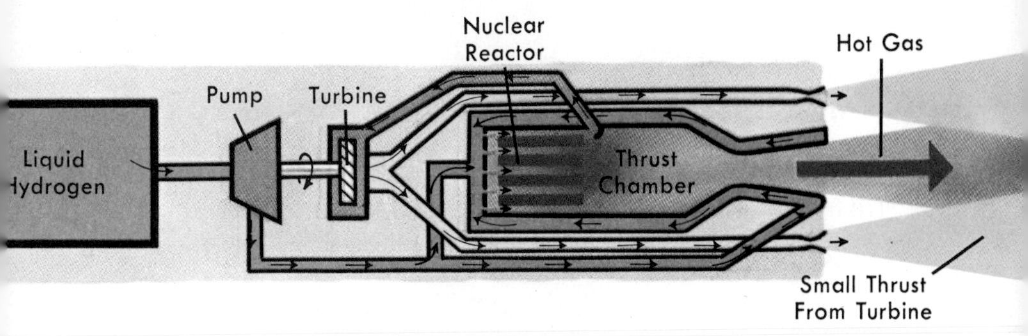

Liquid hydrogen is pumped from its tank. Some of it is pushed through the walls of the thrust chamber to cool the walls. Most of it flows into the thrust chamber where it is heated by a nuclear reactor. The hot gas rushes out of the chamber through the nozzle, creating thrust. A small amount of this vapor is used to drive the turbine, which powers the pump, which keeps the hydrogen flowing to the thrust chamber.

engine does not burn anything. The hot exhaust gas is produced by heating a *single* propellant with a bathtub-size nuclear reactor. The hot propellant gas is accelerated to exhaust speed through a regular exhaust nozzle.

This amounts to replacing the heat from chemical combustion with the heat from a nuclear reactor. The lightest propellant is the best, and nuclear rockets will use hydrogen. It will be carried as a liquid in a single tank. The liquid hydrogen will be forced into the reactor chamber by a pump and there heated to 4,500° F. by the reactor. This is less than the combustion temperature of LOX and kerosene. Despite this the ISP, the specific impulse, will be twice that of a chemical rocket—about eight hundred pounds of thrust for one second using one pound of hydrogen. This is an exhaust speed of twenty thousand miles per hour!

In astronautics, solving one problem usually creates a new one. The nuclear rocket engine is no exception to this rule. Of the many problems that it creates, the most difficult and dangerous is that of nuclear radiation. The crew must be protected from its deadly effects and this means that *shielding* must be used—which means extra weight. Another problem is created by the exhaust gases which may be dangerous. And then, too, the reactor must be controlled. All of these and other problems will be solved. The quiet of the Nevada desert has already been broken by the roar of a nuclear rocket engine.

One of the great advantages of the orbit-to-orbit spaceship is the very low thrust required. With no resistance, it can speed up under the tiniest thrust. Since weight has no meaning, the engine could be large and bulky. It need only produce a small thrust, but again use as little propellant as possible.

These needs are exactly filled by the ion rocket engine. The ion engine achieves exhaust speeds of 400,000 miles per hour! It does this by electrically accelerating tiny charged particles called ions. Ions are atoms which have lost an electron. They can then be accelerated electrically to enormous speeds. To create the ions and to speed them up requires a lot of electrical power. And that is where the nuclear reactor comes in!

An ion rocket engine for an orbit-to-orbit ship will have many parts, most of them heavy. First there will be a nuclear reactor to supply heat energy. A combination of a turbine, radiator, and pump will use the heat energy to drive an electrical generator. The electrical energy from the generator will have two uses. Part of it will be used to "break off" electrons to form ions. The rest will be used to electrically accelerate them in an exhaust jet.

The propellant will be a rare chemical element called cesium. It is used because, of all the elements, it is the most easily ionized. It will be pumped from a storage tank to a heated plate. The hot plate will remove an electron from each cesium atom. Finally the cesium ions will be

An ion rocket engine is made up of many parts. Shown here is just the thrust chamber. Liquid cesium is pumped through heated coils which turn the cesium into vapor. The vapor then passes through a special grid which removes an electron from each cesium atom, turning the atoms into ions. The ions are speeded up into a high speed jet by electrical coils.

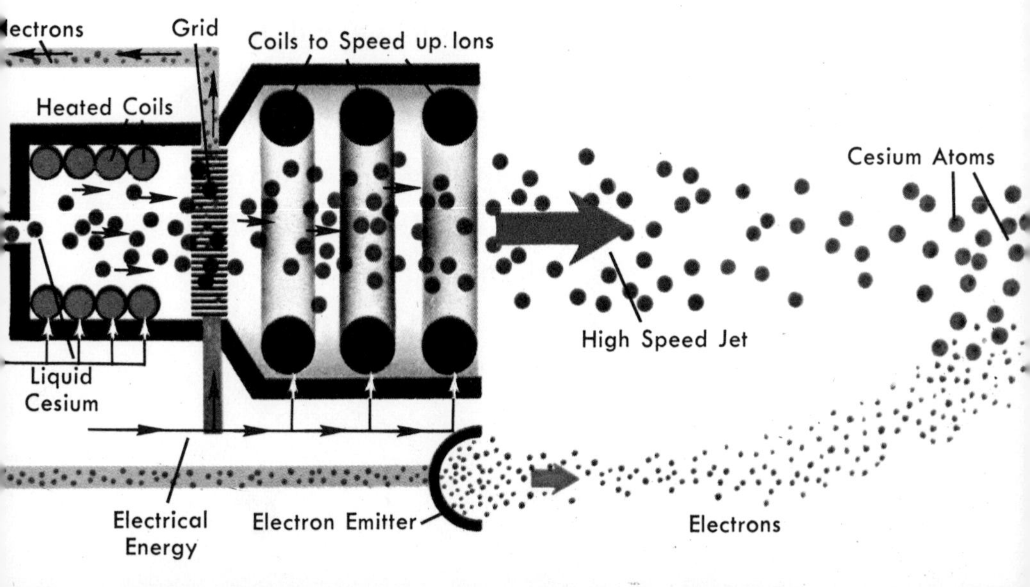

hurled out through the electrical nozzle.

Electrons, removed from the cesium atoms, will also be hurled out into space. There they will rejoin the ions, to form complete atoms. If this were not done, electrons which have a negative charge would build up inside the ship. In time the negatively charged ship would be attracted to the cloud of positively charged ions left behind in space. This would decrease the speed of the ship.

The ion engine is of use only in outer space. The thrust it develops is a tiny fraction of its own weight. An ion engine producing one hundred pounds thrust would weigh about 100,000 pounds! But this is not a difficulty in gravity-free space. What counts is the small amount of propellant it uses. The ion engine needs to use only a trickle of propellant in producing its feeble thrust.

With the use of these two new engines, manned space flight will become a realistic and practical undertaking. The exploration of Mars, for example, will no longer be a great and dangerous gamble.

Remember back to the eight-man Mars expedition: Using chemical rocket engines meant that *twelve hundred* tons of supplies had to be lifted into orbit. This required *one hundred* Earth-to-orbit trips.

If an ion engine were used to thrust the Mars ship through space only *two hundred* tons of supplies would

Parts of our Mars spaceship will be lifted into orbit around the Earth, built, and launched from there. You can see why an ion rocket engine would be best to power the Mars ship. And you can see why nuclear powered cargo rockets will be invaluable in lifting supplies into orbit.

be needed in orbit. And if the cargo rockets were powered by 1½-million-pound thrust chemical booster engines, the number of Earth-to-orbit trips would drop to sixteen. The combination of a sixty-pound thrust ion engine and a 1½-million-pound thrust chemical booster engine would allow the exploration of Mars.

Even more amazing is the effect of the nuclear rocket engine. If the cargo rockets were powered by 1½-million-pound thrust nuclear engines, only four Earth-to-orbit trips could launch the expedition.

"It is a wise man who knows—what he does not know." That is an old saying, but one which applies to both astronautics and this book. Its contents are only a tiny part of the story of astronautics.

Radio communication in space, guidance and control of the spaceship, re-entry into the Earth's atmosphere, protection of the astronauts, space navigation—these are but a few of the many parts that remain for you to learn about.

These then are the engines and spaceships of the future. They will be familiar and commonplace within ten years, for they are being designed and tested at this very moment.

But astronautics never stands still. Better engines and ships will always be needed. The conquest of space will always depend upon men who dream and think and build.

Your dreams may be the ones which will help men reach the stars!

USA
4

WHAT IS MOON MILK?

HOW DO ENGINES WORK?

HOW DEEP CAN DIVERS GO?

Whitman
Learn About Books

THE MICROSCOPE AND A HIDDEN WORLD TO EXPLORE *Irene S. Pyszkowski*

Learn how man discovered the hidden world of the invisible. Find out how microscopes are used by detectives, scientists, doctors, and how it is possible to see tiny living things all around us.

ASTRONOMY—OUR SOLAR SYSTEM AND BEYOND *Robert I. Johnson*

Find out about the planets and moons that circle our star, the Sun. Look at actual photographs of craters on the moon, giant tornadoes on the Sun, and exploding stars millions of miles away from us.

ADVENTURES IN SCIENCE *Charles D. Neal*

Experiments to be done at home show how sound, heat, and light travel . . . why lemon juice can be used to write secret messages . . . why a can heated in just the right way crumples when it cools—and much more.

FIND OUT! FIRST STEP TO THE FUTURE *Dr. Dan Q. Posin*

Have you ever wondered how a telescope works? Or how storms happen? Or how the big electronic brains work? Or how atoms join to make all things on Earth—and in space? Dr. Posin has the answers!

ROCKETS TO EXPLORE THE UNKNOWN *Don E. Rogers*

Learn how rockets, and cannons—and bicycles!—are all a little alike. Find out how rockets work, and how they are being designed to fly faster and farther, to carry man out into unknown space.

BOOKS IN THE LEARN ABOUT SERIES

THE AIRPORT, OUR LINK TO THE SKY
Robert Sidney Bowen

ANIMALS OF THE FIELD AND FOREST
Mina Lewiton

BIRDS AROUND US
Marjorie Stuart

FLOWERS AND WHAT THEY ARE
Mary Elting

TREES AND HOW THEY GROW
Katharine Carter

OUR EARTH, WHAT IT IS
Frederick H. Pough

ROCKS AND WHAT THEY TELL US
Lester del Rey

RIVERS, WHAT THEY DO
Nancy Larrick and Alexander Crosby

PHYSICS, ITS MARVELS AND MYSTERIES
Dr. Daniel Q. Posin

THE BIG BUILDERS
E. Joseph Dreany

TURN TO THE SEA
Athelstan Spilhaus

CAVES AND THEIR MYSTERIES
James McClurg

ENGINES, PROGRESS AND POWER
Don E. Rogers

YOUR BODY
Harry Swartz, M.D.